W9-BUA-143

WITHDRAWN
CHARLESTON COUNTY LIBRARY

GO FOR THE MOON

A ROCKET, A BOY, AND THE FIRST MOON LANDING

CHRIS GALL

ROARING BROOK PRESS

NEW YORK

For B.

Copyright © 2019 by Chris Gall
Published by Roaring Brook Press
Roaring Brook Press is a division of Holtzbrinck Publishing Holdings Limited Partnership
175 Fifth Avenue, New York, NY 10010
mackids.com
All rights reserved

Library of Congress Control Number: 2018955854
ISBN: 978-1-250-15579-5

Our books may be purchased in bulk for promotional, educational, or business use. Please
contact your local bookseller or the Macmillan Corporate and Premium Sales Department
at (800) 221-7945 ext. 5442 or by email at MacmillanSpecialMarkets@macmillan.com.

First edition, 2019
Printed in China by Toppan Leefung Printing Ltd., Dongguan City, Guangdong Province
1   3   5   7   9   10   8   6   4   2

The Moon is out tonight.

In the morning, three brave men will climb inside a giant rocket, blast off into space, and fly to the Moon. And for the first time ever, people will try to walk on it. I'm so excited that I can't sleep!

The astronauts are ready
for the mission, and so am I.

Weeks ago, I started building my rocket. It is small. I had to read the instructions very carefully. Everything has to fit together perfectly or it will not fly.

Our television screen has no color, only black and white. The picture jumps, and sometimes it looks like snow. The reporters said that the astronauts are preparing carefully. They will need a huge amount of **thrust** to leave Earth.

Thrust lifts the rocket off the ground and away from Earth's gravity. The heavier the rocket, the more thrust is needed.

The main engine on the Moon rocket provides 1.5 million pounds of thrust. That means the engine is able to lift 1.5 million pounds into the air. But the rocket to the Moon weighs 6.2 million pounds, or as much as 400 elephants.

So it will need five engines to lift it off the ground.

The giant rocket that will take the astronauts to the Moon is called the Saturn V (pronounced Saturn Five). It is 363 feet tall.

After I built my rocket, I practiced jumping to see how far away from the ground I could go. I am using thrust to jump in the air, but Earth's gravity pulls me down.

The Saturn V rocket has three sections, or stages, stacked together. Each has its own set of engines and functions as a separate rocket. When a stage runs out of propellant, it will be left behind, making the Saturn V lighter. A lighter rocket needs less propellant and can fly farther with its payload, which is the astronauts, their spacecraft, and their Moon lander.

When the first stage runs out of propellant, it is left behind to fall into the ocean.

The same thing happens to the second stage.

At the Kennedy Space Center in Florida, the stages are stacked together in a huge building with the help of a giant crane. The crane can lift 500,000 pounds, or the weight of thirty large bulldozers. The person who operates the crane has to be very careful.

In order to qualify for the job, they have to prove that they can lower a practice section onto an egg without cracking it.

The third stage takes the payload into space . . .

and pushes it to the Moon.

I transported my rocket outside to the launchpad. My rocket is little, but I still have to be careful.

Months before, after it was assembled, the Saturn V was moved to the launchpad. A giant machine called "the crawler" was driven under the rocket and the launch tower. It moved very slowly—it took about six hours to move the rocket three miles to the pad.

The Saturn V engines create thrust by burning the propellant. The hot gases shooting from the giant nozzles will lift the rocket into the air.

The engines do not burn gasoline like a car, but a mixture of kerosene and oxygen in the first stage.

Engine

Rocket body

Oxygen

Kerosene

Hydrogen

Oxygen

My rocket uses water as a propellant. I filled the tank, then I pumped the rocket full of air. When the air is squeezed, it is called **compression**. The compressed air will force the water out to provide thrust, and then the rocket will lift into the air.

Air

Water

The upper two stages burn oxygen and hydrogen, a very light, very explosive gas.

On the morning of the launch, I have a good breakfast of eggs and bacon and my favorite orange drink, called Tang. It is getting close to countdown! I need to get my little astronauts on board.

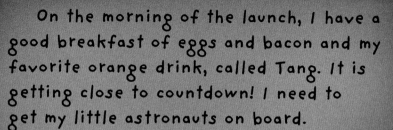

The Saturn V astronauts have their own breakfast early in the morning. Then they are sent to a special room to get into their space suits. They need help.

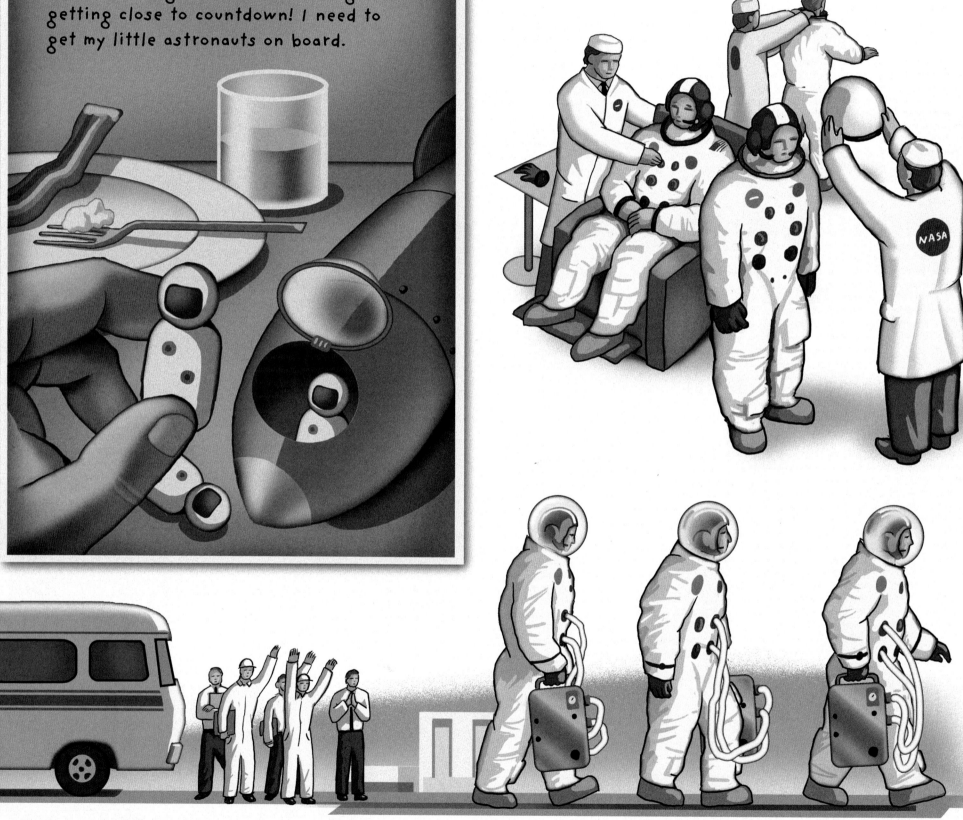

The special suitcases they carry will give them oxygen to breathe until their capsule is safely in space.

Three hours before liftoff, they
ride to the launch tower and take
the elevator to the top of the
Saturn V. It is high above
the ground.

The people who help the astronauts along the way to and from the Moon are in a building called Mission Control in Houston, Texas. They can talk to the astronauts and check all the systems of the spacecraft from far away using radio signals. This is called *telemetry*. Because Earth is always turning, and the rocket will be moving, they have to put antennas all over the world—even on ships and planes.

My brother confirms we are GO FOR LAUNCH.
We are GO FOR THE MOON.

To get to the Moon, the Saturn V must be steered in the right direction. But the Moon is moving around Earth, so it does not stay in one place. It's like if my brother kicks a soccer ball and I throw a stone to try to hit the ball while it is flying through the air. This is how hard it is to land on the Moon without flying past it!

When the astronauts are safely circling, or *orbiting*, Earth, they check all their equipment to make sure everything is working properly.

The direction and speed of the spacecraft are measured from the ground. This is called navigation and guidance. To check the results from Mission Control, the astronauts use a special instrument called a sextant to find their position—just as sailors did long ago to guide their way across the oceans.

Early sailor's sextant

After they have orbited Earth nearly twice, the third stage is reignited to push the astronauts away from Earth's gravity and toward the Moon. In three days, the Moon's gravity will be stronger.

I climb through the hatch of my spaceship. Until I get to the Moon, this will be my home. I bring food and water and power for the trip. I even pack a jar of Tang.

The vehicle that will take the astronauts and the Moon lander all the way to the Moon is made of two parts—one (the service module) with a large engine, and one (the command module) that the astronauts will live and return to Earth in.

The astronauts name the vehicle *Columbia*.

Cooling radiator

The command and service modules are like a very small house. They carry everything the astronauts will need on their journey—food, air, water, and power. They also shield them from the cold of space.

Electricity comes from fuel cells in the service module. They combine hydrogen and oxygen, which creates electricity. The electricity charges the batteries on board. The fuel cells also create lots of water, both for the astronauts to drink and to cool the spacecraft.

Drogue parachute

Docking probe

Hatch

Main parachute

Sextant

Aft equipment bay

Lower equipment bay

Fuel cell

The command module is not designed to land on the Moon. A separate landing vehicle called the lunar module is safely tucked into the top of the third-stage rocket. The astronauts have nicknamed it *Eagle*.

The astronauts ignite explosives to cut Columbia *free from the third stage.*

They turn Columbia *around by using several mini-rockets on the outside of the ship.*

Then they use the rockets to push the nose of Columbia *into the hatch at the top of* Eagle *to pull it away from the third stage. The two craft are connected with latches. This is called docking.*

Lunar module

Docking probe

Command module

Drogue

Latches

Now the astronauts can go from one ship to the other. Together, they coast all the way to the Moon.

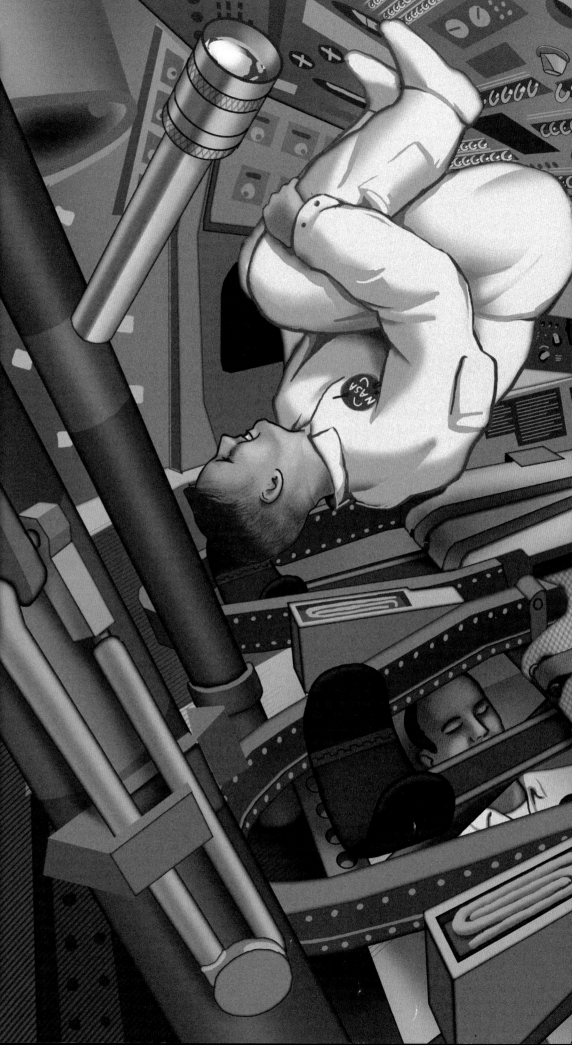

I eat my snacks from a plastic bag, and I sip my Tang through a straw. I make sure I don't spill anything, because in space there is no gravity. Any spills will float around inside the ship and cause trouble for the spacecraft and the astronauts.

The astronauts sleep when they can, but it is not easy because there are many noises inside the spacecraft. They eat food that's just like food on Earth, but it's dried out so it will weigh less. Water is added from a special water gun when it is time to eat.

The next day, I get to know my lunar module.
I have to climb a ladder to get in and out of it.
It has no seats, so we have to stand to see out
the windows.

Radar antenna

Ascent engine

Oxidizer tank

Fuel tank

Descent engine

Eagle has two parts. The lower part has its own engine, which is used to slow down *Eagle* as it approaches the surface of the Moon. The legs are extended before departing from the command service module and have large round pads in case the ground is very soft.

The upper part also has an engine and room for two astronauts. It will carry them to the Moon's surface and back to the command module after the landing.

It is time to put on my space suit!

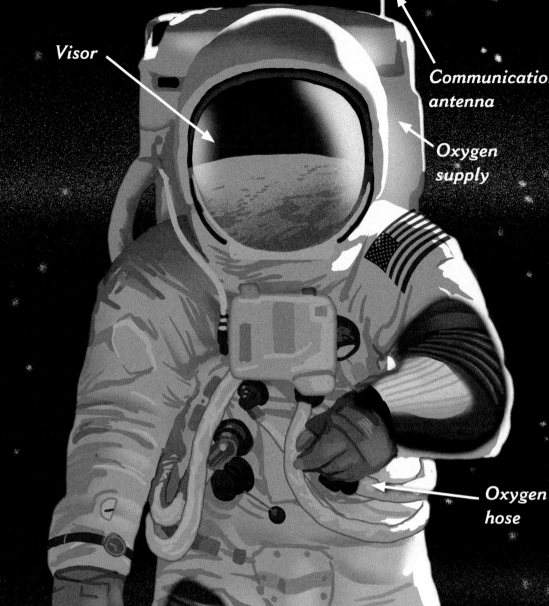

Visor

Communicatio
antenna

Oxygen
supply

Oxygen
hose

Inner suit

Lunar boots

The astronauts' suits are like small spaceships. The Moon has no air, so they have a special backpack that gives them oxygen to breathe and water for cooling. The suit is made of many layers. The first layer has hundreds of feet of tubing that carries water to cool the body. The next layer keeps the air inside, and the outer layer provides protection from heat and cold. Also, the suits are easy to move in.

After *Columbia* has orbited the Moon several times, astronauts Neil Armstrong and Buzz Aldrin say goodbye to Michael Collins. He will stay behind in *Columbia* and wait for them to return. Neil and Buzz climb aboard *Eagle*, close the hatch, and undock from *Columbia*.

Landing on the Moon isn't easy. The astronauts aim to land at a place called the Sea of Tranquillity. It isn't a real sea, because there is no water on the Moon.

To get there they have to steer *Eagle* exactly, with just the right amount of thrust to slow down *Eagle* so they don't crash. The astronauts fire their engine to slowly drop closer to the Moon's surface.

I send my lunar-module model down a piece of string. If the lunar module goes down too fast, it will crash. If it goes down too slowly, it will run out of fuel and also crash! The string needs to be at just the right angle.

A small computer controls *Eagle*. When they get closer to the Moon's surface, Neil guides the computer to a safe landing spot. Carefully, he inches toward the surface of the Moon. He does not want to land in a crater.

Then, with a soft bump, *Eagle* lands on the Moon.

My whole family huddles around the TV. Everyone is so nervous that no one speaks. Finally, I see a shadow moving across the screen. On the TV I hear: "That's one small step for a man, one giant leap for mankind." Neil Armstrong is the first man to walk on the Moon! Buzz Aldrin climbs down the ladder next.

I run around the house practicing my giant leaps. With the Moon shining brightly overhead, I bound outside like a real astronaut.

The astronauts spend two and a half hours on the surface of the Moon. They collect rocks, take pictures, and set up experiments. The Moon has much less gravity than Earth, so an astronaut needs less effort to hop around. They jump like little kids.

But soon it is time to go home. They leave their backpacks on the Moon because they will not need them again. And they no longer need the landing section of the lunar module, so it is also left behind.

Neil and Buzz ignite *Eagle*'s engine and blast off the Moon. Soon, they carefully dock *Eagle* to *Columbia*. They bring some rocks and their pictures with them.

LUNAR SAMPLE RETURN

Then they detach *Eagle* and aim for Earth the same way that they aimed for the Moon. They use the thrust from *Columbia*'s main engine to push them out of orbit and away from the Moon's gravity. Soon, Earth's gravity will become stronger, and after three days, their journey will be almost over. Then they will be near home.

The empty *Eagle* falls slowly back to the Moon, where eventually it crashes and creates a crater.

When *Columbia* nears Earth, it
is time to say goodbye to the service
module. The two parts of the spacecraft
separate with a bang.

The astronauts use little rockets
to turn *Columbia* around so its
large, round heat shield is pointed
toward Earth.

When an object passes through air
at a high speed, the air is compressed
in front of it and gets very hot. When
Columbia reaches Earth's atmosphere,
this shockwave will become almost as
hot as the surface of the sun.

The heat shield
prevents it from burning up. The
vehicle must enter the atmosphere
at just the right angle or it will skip
away into space.

When *Columbia* reaches ten thousand feet above the ocean, it has slowed enough and the main parachutes shoot out of its nose. Soon it lands safely in the sea with a terrific splash. Big balloons keep *Columbia* upright.

The astronauts are home safe. They have traveled five hundred thousand miles to do what no human has ever done before. Thousands of men and women on Earth helped them get to the Moon. Soon there will be parades and hugs and tears of joy.

Back in Florida at the Kennedy Space Center, a new rocket is being prepared and new astronauts are training. The next countdown starts.

At home, the countdown has started, too.

My next journey has just begun.

AUTHOR'S NOTE

On July 20, 1969, at nine in the evening, I sat transfixed in front of a snowy black-and-white television in a small farmhouse in rural Illinois. The dark shapes on the screen were hard to make out, and the wait had been long. Neil Armstrong was about to descend the ladder of the lunar module and set foot on the Moon. In that moment, my life's path would be forever changed. I was seven years old.

Astronomy and space travel were my first true passions. I built all the models from the Apollo program. I spent every clear night in my front yard, peering through an antique telescope and hoping to see something that no one had ever seen before. I launched small rockets propelled by compressed water. By the time I was twelve, I had built my first rocket that actually burned solid rocket fuel. In subsequent years, I built many more, all with different flight characteristics, allowing me to go even higher and faster. My interest in rocketry continues to this day.

While I was never able to actually propel myself into space, I was eventually able to find a way to get off the ground. I earned my pilot's license as soon as I had the money to do so, and I eventually embarked on the pursuit of the crowning achievement of any aspiring model maker: I built my own aircraft. Not a model, but a real plane that I could fly.

I still have my rockets, though some are now old and fragile and will never fly again. Many flew to great heights. Some smashed to pieces when the parachutes failed. And a few left Earth with a shattering roar, soaring higher and higher until they were way out of sight, never to be seen again. I like to think that one of them made it to the Moon.

FUN FACTS

The first liquid-fueled rocket was invented by Robert Goddard in 1926.

Surfboard makers were employed to help design the insulation between the fuel tanks because they had better knowledge of lightweight foam cells.

Early test models of the command module were dropped from towers into pools of water to test the strength of the capsule design. The first model promptly sank.

Hamburger buns were banned on board because the crumbs could get into delicate instruments.

As the command module flew to the Moon, the sun would heat the sunny side of the ship to dangerously hot levels. The spaceship had to rotate slowly to equally distribute the heat on all sides. It was called Barbecue Mode.

An iPhone has more computing power than all the computers NASA used during the Apollo program.

The walls of the lunar module were slightly thicker than aluminum foil. The lander had to be as light as possible, and the spacecraft did not have to hold much air pressure. Astronauts had to take great care not to puncture the walls.

The Apollo 11 mission utilized 400,000 engineers, technicians, and scientists.

Most of the lunar module was covered in Mylar to reflect the sun's hot rays. It had to be lightweight. Mylar is the same material used in party balloons.

Early suit designs inflated like a balloon when pressurized with air. The astronauts could not move in them.

Without space suits, in the vacuum of space, moisture on and inside the astronauts' bodies would boil. The oxygen in their cells would fatally expand, also causing their blood to boil.

The company that made space suits for the astronauts had only made women's underwear before the space program.

Five hundred million viewers around the world tuned in to watch the first steps on the Moon.

GLOSSARY

Astronaut
A person who travels in space

Atmosphere
The air we breathe, which is mostly nitrogen and oxygen

Compression
The force used to make something smaller

Docking
Connecting two spaceships

Gravity
A force between objects that draws them together

Hydrogen
A very light gas that is highly flammable

Kerosene
A flammable fuel first used in lamps

Orbit
A path of an object in space around another object of greater mass

Oxygen
The gas that our bodies need to live

Tang
An instant orange drink supposedly favored by astronauts

Telemetry
The transmission of signals containing information between ground and spaceship

Thrust
The force that moves an object

SOURCES

Baker, David. *Apollo 13 Owners' Workshop Manual*. Zenith, 2013.

Chaikin, Andrew. *A Man on the Moon: The Voyages of the Apollo Astronauts*. Viking, 1994.

NASA. *Saturn V Flight Manual*, Periscope Film LLC, 2011.

nasa.gov

Riley, Christopher, and Nick Davidson, dir. *Moon Machines*. 2009; Discovery-Gaiam. DVD.

Smithsonian Institution 3-D digital model of the command module: 3d.si.edu/apollo11cm

Ward, Jonathan H. *Rocket Ranch: The Nuts and Bolts of the Apollo Moon Program at Kennedy Space Center*. Springer, 2015.

Woods, David. *NASA Saturn V 1967–1973 (Apollo 4 to Apollo 17 & Skylab) Owners' Workshop Manual*. Haynes Publishing, 2016.

Woods, W. David. *How Apollo Flew to the Moon*. Springer, 2008. (Thank you for the soccer ball example, page 20.)

ACKNOWLEDGMENTS

Special thanks to David Woods for his careful proofreading of this book.

PLACES TO VISIT

airandspace.si.edu

visitnasa.com

spacecamp.com/space/academy